LIMERICKS

BY YVONNE PEARSON

ILLUSTRATED BY KATHLEEN PETELINSEK

Published by The Child's World®
1980 Lookout Drive · Mankato, MN 56003-1705
800-599-READ · www.childsworld.com

ACKNOWLEDGMENTS
The Child's World®: Mary Berendes, Publishing Director
Red Line Editorial: Editorial direction
The Design Lab: Design and production

Photographs ©: Agita Leimane/Thinkstock, 8; Thinkstock,
13; Hill Street Studios/Thinkstock, 14; Vent Studios/
Shutterstock Images, 19

ISBN 9781631436963
LCCN 2014945438

Printed in the United States of America
Mankato, MN
November, 2014
PA02240

About the Author

Yvonne Pearson is a poet and a social worker. She has published many poems and won contests. She writes essays and books, too. She lives in Minneapolis, Minnesota. She also lives in California near her grandchildren part of each year. Her Web site is *www.yvonnepearson.com*.

About the Illustrator

Kathleen Petelinsek is a graphic designer and illustrator. She has been designing and illustrating books for children for 20 years. She lives in Minnesota with her husband, two dogs, a cat, and three fancy chickens.

TABLE OF CONTENTS

What Is a Poem?

Limericks are a type of poetry. Poems are a special kind of writing. Have you ever memorized the words to a song? You were memorizing a poem!

Poems are different than other kinds of writing. Poems are often written in lines. A line can be a complete thought, like a sentence. But a line can also be as short as one word.

The words in a line are arranged to make pleasing or fun sounds. Sometimes poems **rhyme**. Sometimes they don't.

But poems almost always have **rhythm**. This is the way the words in a poem sound together. Rhythm makes poems feel like music. In fact, many songs are poems set to music. To make rhythm, each line has a pattern of **syllables**, or single sounds. Syllables can be **stressed** or unstressed.

Dog is a single syllable, or sound. *Boy* is also a single syllable. *Chick-en* has two syllables. Clap your hands as you say a word. This helps you count the word's syllables!

A stressed syllable is the part of a word you say a bit louder. For example, say, "Go out*side*." The last syllable, *side*, sounds louder than *out*. *Side* is stressed.

Poems can be about anything. People often use poetry to talk about feelings. Poets also write poems to describe an action or event. You could write a poem about an everyday activity, such as playing ball with your dog. Or a special event, such as Fourth of July fireworks.

People often use poetry to have fun. You get to play with words when you write a poem. The famous poet Robert Frost called poetry "serious play."

WHAT IS A LIMERICK?

Limericks are written especially for fun. Limericks make playing with words easy. They have a bouncy rhythm.

Some people think these poems got their name from a town in Ireland called Limerick. Some of the oldest limericks were Mother Goose nursery rhymes, like "Hickory, Dickory, Dock." They were put in a book called *Mother Goose's Melody* in approximately 1781. Then a poet named Edward Lear made limericks famous in his book, *The Book of Nonsense*, in 1846. Limericks are almost always funny. Some are very silly.

Limerick is a very old town. It has been around for more than 1,000 years!

A cow once jumped over the moon.
She jumped just a moment too soon.
She started to flop
As she rounded the top,
She bounced like a giant balloon.

?

How many syllables are in the first line of this limerick?

CHAPTER TWO

2

Limerick Sounds

To make limericks work, poets have to follow some rules. All limericks have five lines. Limericks also rhyme in a certain way. A rhyme is when the endings of two words sound alike. For example, *cat* and *bat* rhyme.

All limericks have the same rhyme pattern. This means the rhyming sounds repeat in a certain order. The different rhymes in a poem are given letters. A limerick rhyme pattern is AABBA. That means lines one, two, and five have

the same rhyme (A). Lines three and four
have a different rhyme (B).

There once was a boy named Ned **A**
Who simply would not go to bed. **A**
The next day at school **B**
He fell off his stool, **B**
Too weary to hold up his head. **A**

The A rhyme words are Ned, bed, *and* head. *The B rhyme words are* school *and* stool.

?

What other words could rhyme with the A rhymes in this limerick?

Rhymes can also be slanted. That's when the words sound similar but don't exactly rhyme. For example, *fish* and *itch* is a **slant rhyme**. *Poet* and *goat* is another slant rhyme.

Make two lists of words that rhyme with one another. The first list can be your A rhymes. The second list will be your B rhymes. Use these lists to write a limerick!

LIMERICKS HAVE RHYTHM

The stressed syllables in a limerick help give it a bouncy rhythm. The rhythm makes you feel like clapping or dancing.

In a limerick, lines one, two, and five have three stressed syllables. Lines three and four have two stressed syllables. Try to clap the rhythm as you say it. Or you could tap your foot to it.

Music also has rhythm. Musical rhythm is the pattern of sounds in a song.

Try reading the poem about Ned out loud. Listen for the stressed syllables.

There ONCE was a BOY named NED
Who SIM-ply would NOT go to BED.
The NEXT day at SCHOOL
He FELL off his STOOL,
Too WEAR-y to HOLD up his HEAD.

Can you feel and hear the rhythm?

Limericks Are Silly

Limericks tell a simple story. But the story doesn't always make much sense. That's because limericks are usually jokes. They are absurd. This means they are very silly. Some limericks might not make any sense. For example, a famous limerick by Edward Lear talks about a man with a beard. Do you know what lived in his beard? Owls, larks, a hen, and a wren.

A limerick usually starts out with the name of a person or a place. The middle of the limerick explains something that happened at the place or to the person. The last line is a surprise or a joke.

There once was a girl named Marie
Who climbed to the top of a tree.
A little bird said,
"I want to be fed."
Marie gave him cookies and tea.

?

What are the A and B rhymes in this limerick?

The limerick about Marie is absurd. It does not really make sense. It begins with the name of a girl, Marie. Then it talks about what happens. She climbs a tree and meets a talking bird. The limerick ends with a silly line.

Some limericks are tongue twisters. This means they use combinations of words that are very hard to say. "She sells seashells by the seashore" is a tongue twister.

The last line of a limerick can be written in three different ways. The words can be completely different from the words in the first line, like in the limericks about Marie and Ned.

The last line can end with the same word as the first line. For example, the poem about Marie could end with, "'You already ate!' said Marie."

The last line can also be almost exactly the same as the first line. Like this: "'Too bad!' said the girl named Marie."

NOW IT'S YOUR TURN!

Writing limericks is fun. You get to play with words and make silly jokes. People have been playing with limericks for hundreds of years. Now that you know more about limericks, it's time to write your own!

TIPS FOR YOUNG POETS

1. Read poems out loud. Tap your foot or bounce up and down to find the rhythm.

2. Listen to other people read poems out loud. Think about whether or not you like the poems. What do you like or dislike about them?

3. Learn some poems by memory.

4. Pick a word, then make a list of words that rhyme with it.

5. Ask someone to make up the first line of a limerick. Write the rest of the limerick using that line. Then write a different limerick using the same line.

6. Try writing a limerick about a person or a place that you know well.

7. Don't worry about making your poem perfect. Have fun when you write poetry. Be as silly as you can.

8. It's OK to break some of the rules when you write a limerick. You can add an extra syllable or leave one out.

GLOSSARY

absurd (ab-ZURD): Something that is very silly or completely ridiculous is absurd. Limericks are often absurd.

rhyme (RIME): Words that rhyme have the same ending sound. The first, second, and fifth lines of a limerick rhyme.

rhythm (RITH-uhm): Rhythm is a repeating pattern of sounds in poetry. Limericks have a steady rhythm.

slant rhyme (SLANT RIME): Two words that sound similar but are not exactly alike have a slant rhyme. *Fox* and *lock* is a slant rhyme.

stressed (STREST): A word or syllable is stressed when it is said a bit stronger or louder than another word or syllable. The pattern of stressed and unstressed words decides a poem's rhythm.

syllables (SIL-uh-buhlz): Syllables are units of sounds in a word. You can tell how many syllables a word has by clapping your hands as you say the word.

TO LEARN MORE

BOOKS

Aaronson, Brent. *All Mixed Up: A Collection of Limericks for Kids.* North Charleston, SC: CreateSpace, 2014.

Bodden, Valerie. *Poetry Basics: Limericks.* Mankato, MN: Creative Education, 2010.

Prelutsky, Jack. *Pizza, Pigs, and Poetry: How to Write a Poem.* New York: Greenwillow Books, 2008.

ON THE WEB

Visit our Web site for lots of links about limericks:
www.childsworld.com/links

Note to Parents, Teachers, and Librarians: We routinely check our Web links to make sure they're safe, active sites—so encourage your readers to check them out!

INDEX